Original title:
A Frosted Dawn

Copyright © 2024 Swan Charm
All rights reserved.

Author: Liina Liblikas
ISBN HARDBACK: 978-9908-52-056-8
ISBN PAPERBACK: 978-9908-52-057-5
ISBN EBOOK: 978-9908-52-058-2

## The Magic of Crystalized Dawn

Glistening light spills from the sky,
Whispers of night bid farewell and sigh.
Frost-kissed leaves in a gentle dance,
Morning greets us with a fleeting glance.

Colors blend in a soft embrace,
Nature dons a crystalline lace.
Each droplet glows, a gem in the sun,
A new day begins, the magic begun.

## Silver Hues in a Winter's Wake

Silver flakes drift on a silent breeze,
Covering branches, their final freeze.
The world transformed in a shimmering shroud,
Nature whispers softly, gentle and proud.

Footprints of dreams on the powdered ground,
In this winter's hush, solace is found.
Every shadow glows, kissed by the light,
In silver hues, the heart takes flight.

## The Frosted Canvas of Tomorrow

Brush strokes of white on a waiting world,
Frosted edges, as dreams are unfurled.
Each morning paints new tales to tell,
In the still of dawn, all is well.

Glittering whispers, secrets in snow,
Tomorrow awaits with possibilities aglow.
Nature's palette, fresh and bright,
Every frost a reminder of light.

## **Enchantment in the Air**

In the cool stillness, magic resides,
Whirls of wonder where spirit abides.
Invisible threads weave stories anew,
Even the air sings of things that are true.

Dancing shadows beneath the pale moon,
Echoing laughter as night sings its tune.
Inhale the whispers, feel the embrace,
Enchantment in the air, a delicate grace.

## Shivering Beams of Gold

In the hush of morning's glow,
Whispers dance on silver streams.
Shivering beams of gold do flow,
Wrapped in gentle, fragile dreams.

Nature holds her breath in calm,
As the day begins to rise.
With each ray, a soothing balm,
Painting colors 'neath the skies.

Golden threads by breezes spun,
Mingle softly with the air.
Underneath the watchful sun,
Beauty blooms, beyond compare.

Time stands still, the world awakes,
Birds begin their morning song.
Life unfolds, as stillness breaks,
In this moment, we belong.

A tapestry of light is cast,
Lifting shadows, chasing night.
Here in stillness, peace holds fast,
Shivering beams in pure delight.

## **Crystalline Dawn's Awakening**

At dawn's first touch, the world awakes,
With crystalline hues in silver light.
Nature stirs, and softly shakes,
Colors dance in morning's sight.

Glistening leaves in sunlight play,
Each drop glows, a fleeting gem.
Whispers of a brand new day,
As the earth begins to stem.

Birds sing sweetly from their nest,
As shadows gently fade away.
In this moment, we are blessed,
Crystalline breaths of light convey.

Winds embrace the waking trees,
Stirring dreams long left behind.
In the air, a gentle breeze,
Carries hopes of humankind.

Every color finds its place,
In the canvas of the sky.
Crystalline dawn, a warm embrace,
Bids the sleeping night goodbye.

## Whispers of the Icy Morning

Morning frost whispers low,
Gentle breath on the ground.
It dances on leaves, aglow,
A world wrapped in silence, profound.

Footsteps crunch with soft might,
Nature wakes, slow and clear.
Birds join the crisp daylight,
Their melodies draw us near.

Shadows stretch with the sun,
As warmth starts to unfold.
Each moment a treasure won,
In the chill, stories told.

The air sparkles with breath,
Frosted dreams weave and spin.
In this stillness, we rest,
A new day about to begin.

Hope rises in the light,
With every hue that we see.
The icy morning, a sight,
Whispers secrets, wild and free.

## **Veils of Silver Light**

Veils of silver softly fall,
Draped over land like lace.
Whispers echo through the hall,
As night leaves without a trace.

Stars blink in the fading dark,
Painting patterns in the sky.
A tranquil world, a silent spark,
Where dreams and shadows lie.

Moonbeams dance on the lake,
Casting light on the still shore.
In the calm, memories wake,
And wander forevermore.

Nature holds her breath tight,
Each moment a fleeting chance.
In the soft embrace of night,
The world begins its dance.

With dawn's first tender ray,
The silver light will depart.
Yet in whispers, it will stay,
An imprint on the heart.

## **The Chill Before Sunlight**

Before the sun breaks the haze,
A chill hangs in the air.
Nature waits in quiet ways,
Painting frost on branches bare.

Stillness wraps the waking day,
As shadows merge with the night.
In this pause, the world at play,
Soft dreams linger, holding tight.

Clouds blush with a hint of gold,
Hints of warmth begin to rise.
In this moment, hearts are bold,
Kindled by the morning skies.

The chill whispers secrets soft,
Of journeys yet to unfold.
In this dance, spirits lift off,
Chasing warmth, brave and bold.

As sunlight breaks through the mist,
All worries fade like a sigh.
In this beautiful twist,
The chill prepares us to fly.

## **Crystals on the Horizon**

Crystals glint on the horizon,
A treasure waiting to be found.
Their shimmer speaks of the season,
In whispers, they dance around.

Morning dew on whispering grass,
Each droplet a fleeting spark.
In sunlight's glow, moments pass,
Painting colors in the dark.

The earth adorned in nature's art,
Each crystal a story untold.
Fragments of light with pure heart,
In the warmth, dreams unfold.

Winds carry tales on their breath,
Of journeys beyond the day.
In this beauty, life finds depth,
As we chase the light's ballet.

On the edge of the dawn's glow,
As colors begin to collide,
Crystals on the horizon flow,
In unity, we take the ride.

## A Dance of Icicles and Light

Icicles glisten in the sun,
Crystal dancers, cold ones run.
They twinkle bright with morning's grace,
In nature's cold, their beauty's place.

Winter whispers in the breeze,
A melody that brings such ease.
Shadows play on snow's white sheet,
As sunlight drapes the world in heat.

Each drop that melts begins to sing,
A song of joy that spring will bring.
With every drip, the rhythm grows,
A symphony in winter's close.

Frozen branches sway and bow,
In this moment, take a vow.
To cherish light in darkest days,
And find the warmth in winter's ways.

So let the dance of light prevail,
In frosty air, where stories sail.
Embrace the chill, the fleeting sight,
Of icicles' joyful, sparkling light.

## **Chilling Echoes at Daybreak**

At dawn, the world is dressed in frost,
A quiet beauty, never lost.
Echoes linger in the pale,
While shadows flee, the night grows frail.

Breath of winter fills the air,
Whispers soft, beyond compare.
Every blade of grass is veiled,
In icy crystals, dreams unveiled.

Birdsong breaks the morning calm,
A gentle tune, a soothing balm.
Nature wakes, her arms stretched wide,
As sunlight spills, the night's denied.

Chilling echoes softly fade,
In the light where hopes are made.
Each moment, fresh like fallen snow,
A canvas pure, where visions flow.

Embrace the cold, the still, the bright,
In this dance of day and night.
Through chilling echoes, life will rise,
Awake to warmth, beneath the skies.

## The Glow of a Frosty Awakening

Morning breaks with frosty breath,
Each branch adorned, a sign of death.
Yet life returns with warming light,
As day unfolds from winter's night.

The ground is crisp beneath my feet,
A frozen quilt, both bright and sweet.
With every step, a crunching sound,
Awakens earth in magic found.

Through icy air, the sun will creep,
And stir the world from winter's sleep.
A glow emerges, soft and warm,
Transforming cold with nature's charm.

In whispered winds, the promise grows,
Of blooms and life where winter froze.
The trees awaken, stretch and yawn,
As day gives way to early dawn.

So let the frosty morning rise,
With hues of gold against the skies.
In every sparkle, find your place,
A frosty glow, a warm embrace.

## Celestial Frost on the Earth

Stars twinkle in the frosty night,
A blanket of diamonds, pure delight.
Moonlight dances on the snow,
A celestial glow, a softened flow.

Frosty patterns grace the trees,
Whispers cool, carried by the breeze.
The world transforms, as shadows blend,
In silver light, where dreams extend.

Every breath is crisp and clear,
Filling the night with warmth and cheer.
Nature sleeps with tender grace,
Wrapped in frost, a soft embrace.

Celestial beauty shines so bright,
Guiding hearts with gentle light.
In the stillness, magic stirs,
As frost paints lines where wonder whirs.

So pause and witness this grand view,
Underneath the midnight blue.
Celestial frost on earth's fair face,
A timeless moment, a sacred space.

## Soft Sparkles of a Cold Awakening

In the dawn's fragile embrace,
Soft sparkles begin to light,
Whispers of frost lace the ground,
Crystals dance in morning's sight.

The air breathes in a quiet chill,
Voices of nature softly hum,
Each flake a delicate story,
As the waking world becomes.

Trees bow with their silver crowns,
A glistening blanket spreads wide,
Each step a crunch beneath feet,
In this serene winter tide.

The sun peeks shyly around,
Painting shadows in cold hues,
As soft sparkles twirl and glide,
Warming hearts with gentle views.

A moment held in timeless grace,
A cold awakening unfolds,
In the silence, beauty speaks,
With soft sparkles, winter holds.

## The Lacework of Light and Ice

Upon the branch, a shimmer hangs,
The lacework of light and ice,
Filigree etched by frosty hands,
Nature's calm, so pure and nice.

Beneath the arch of frosted air,
A delicate web weaves its thread,
Sunlight kisses the winter fair,
Where shadows of magic tread.

Each droplet sways in harmony,
A crystal song the breeze will make,
The world adorned in reverie,
In this stillness, hearts awake.

Contrasts blend with gentle grace,
An invitation to behold,
The splendor of this tranquil space,
Whispers of winter, stories told.

With every breath, the world exhales,
Emboldened by this winter's lull,
The lacework of light unveils,
An artful tapestry so full.

## Awakened by a Silver Mist

At dawn, a silver mist appears,
Cloaked in whispers, soft and white,
Nature sighs and stretches slow,
Welcoming the tender light.

With a brush of gentle hand,
The world transforms, a quiet spell,
Everything wrapped in quiet dreams,
A tranquil peace where spirits dwell.

Echoes of water dance nearby,
Rippling softly through the dawn,
As if the earth hums in reply,
To the awakening of the morn.

In the hush so thick and sweet,
The silver mist starts to lift,
A canvas pure, a symphony,
In which the day feels like a gift.

Awake, the world now stirs to life,
Framed in silver, all aglow,
A moment caught in misty light,
Where beauty whispers soft and low.

## The Prelude of Crisp Warmth

Amidst the chill of waking night,
A prelude of warmth begins to rise,
Soft hues of dawn break through,
Beneath the vast, awakening skies.

Crimson flush and amber rays,
Draw the shadows from their rest,
Nature stirs in quiet phase,
Holding dreams close to her chest.

Each breath carries a hint of sun,
A promise wrapped in golden glow,
As frost melts slowly, one by one,
The world unfolds in gentle flow.

With whispers of a brand new day,
The earth revives, the heart ignites,
In the chorus of soft sun's play,
The warmth unfurls, the world ignites.

In this dance of light and shade,
The prelude sings, a tune divine,
As warmth envelops every glade,
In harmony, the day will shine.

## Shivering Dawn's Tender Touch

Soft light spills on waking ground,
Whispers of the night unbound.
Frosty breath of dawn's embrace,
Kisses gently every space.

Birds awaken, chirps abound,
Nature's melody profound.
Trees adorned in silver lace,
Drawing life from every place.

The world blinks in early light,
Shadows fade, revealing sight.
Gentle warmth begins to spread,
Chasing off the night's cold dread.

Each petal shines, a sparkling dew,
Morning's grace in every hue.
With every sigh, the day takes flight,
Comfort found in dawn's sweet light.

With every ray, new hope is spun,
The shivering dawn has just begun.
Embracing all, it gently flows,
In tender touch, the daylight grows.

## A Silent Canvas of Light

Morning hues, soft and bright,
Paint the world in gentle light.
Each shadow whispers lingering dreams,
On this canvas, silence beams.

Waves of color dance serene,
Nature's brush, a timeless scene.
Clouds drift slowly, pure and white,
Woven threads of day and night.

Fields of gold, so vast and wide,
Glowing softly as they bide.
Gentle whispers fill the air,
In stillness crafted with great care.

A rabbit hops, a deer stands tall,
Life awakens, answering the call.
Each breath taken, a subtle song,
In this silence, we belong.

With each stroke, the world anew,
A masterpiece in every view.
The sun ascends, the night takes flight,
On this silent canvas of light.

## The Icebound Awakening

Frozen tears on windows weep,
Nature lies in icy sleep.
Silvery whispers fill the air,
A quiet stillness everywhere.

Branches strong with frost adorned,
By winter's chill they are transformed.
The world beneath a crystal sheet,
In this magic, life discreet.

Yet within, a stirring lies,
Beneath the cold, a spark defies.
Roots grip tight, in silent wait,
For warmth to break the frozen fate.

Each morning brings a subtle spark,
Sunrise glimmers through the dark.
And as the thaw begins to show,
The icebound heart starts to glow.

From the stillness, life will rise,
Underneath the winter skies.
In the thaw, new dreams awake,
From icebound depths, the earth will shake.

## When the World Turns to Crystal

A hush falls over every lane,
As winter weaves its frosty chain.
The world transformed, a dazzling sight,
Glistening gently in pure white.

Each breath of wind, a phantom sigh,
Frozen echoes that drift and fly.
Frosted dreams on rooftops rest,
In this wonder, nature's best.

Icicles dangle, sharp and clear,
Their beauty sharp, yet full of fear.
With every step, a crunch, a thrill,
In this crystal world, hearts stand still.

The sun descends, a fiery glaze,
Turns the ice to fiery praise.
Shimmering shards, a sparkling view,
Wrapped in magic, every hue.

When the world turns to crystal bright,
In the stillness of the night.
Nature's beauty, bold and fine,
Leaves us yearning to entwine.

## **When Time Stands in Silver Stillness**

In quiet moments, shadows blend,
Whispers of the night descend.
Stars above, they softly sigh,
While dreams like silver streams drift by.

Frozen echoes, the world holds tight,
Embracing peace, devoid of light.
The moon a guardian, high and bright,
In silver stillness, hearts take flight.

Moments linger, soft and clear,
Time stands still, nothing to fear.
In whispered breaths, the night unfolds,
A tale of silver, softly told.

Caught in time, a gentle flow,
Where secrets of the night bestow.
In every pause, life finds its grace,
In silver stillness, we embrace.

With each heartbeat, echoes play,
Telling stories of yesterday.
As dawn approaches, shadows fade,
Yet in this stillness, love is made.

## **Glistening Hopes of the New Light**

Awakening hues in morning's glow,
Glistening hopes in the world below.
Bright petals dance in gentle winds,
A symphony of life begins.

With every ray that breaks the dark,
A spark ignites, a tender arc.
Nature's chorus lifts the soul,
In the dawn, we find our role.

Promises bloom in vibrant fields,
As hope's embrace the heart yields.
Dew-kissed dreams on blades of grass,
Each moment cherished, none shall pass.

Through the trees, a soft breeze weaves,
Whispers of trust the heart believes.
In the soft light of dawn's caress,
Glistening hopes, our souls confess.

As shadows vanish, brightening skies,
With opened hearts, we see the wise.
Together we rise, hand in hand,
Glistening hopes across the land.

## **The First Light's Frosted Laugh**

The first light breaks, a frosty glow,
Whispers of winter start to flow.
Snowflakes twirl in the gentle breeze,
Nature's laughter among the trees.

Cold air sparkles, the dawn ignites,
With shimmering layers, pure delights.
Every branch, a crystal trace,
In laughter's dance, we find our place.

As frost unfolds, a hush descends,
Time stands still; the stillness bends.
Sunlight kisses the icy ground,
In every glimmer, joy is found.

With each heartbeat, winter sighs,
The world awakes, the spirit flies.
In the frosted air, we come alive,
The first light's laugh, our souls revive.

In this moment, magic thrives,
In winter's heart, where beauty dives.
The world aglow with laughter bright,
In every shimmer, pure delight.

## In the Heart of Winter's Glow

In the heart where shadows play,
Winter's glow leads the way.
Softly falling, the silvery white,
Wraps the earth in tranquil light.

Beneath the frost, life stirs anew,
Silent whispers of dreams in hue.
A cozy warmth in the coldest air,
Bringing hearts together, a love affair.

With each breath, we feel the chill,
Yet in this stillness, time stands still.
In winter's embrace, we find our rest,
In its glow, we are truly blessed.

Snowflakes twinkle, like stars descends,
In every flake, a story bends.
As laughter echoes through the trees,
In the heart of winter, we find peace.

When night falls, the world ignites,
With twinkling gems of frosty lights.
In shadows cast, our spirits grow,
In the heart of winter's glow.

## Dawn's Crystal Spectacle

The sun peeks through the trees,
Casting light on dew-kissed leaves.
Colors burst across the sky,
Nature wakes with a soft sigh.

Birds begin their gentle song,
Echoing where they belong.
Clouds reflect a rosy hue,
Whispers dance with morning's dew.

The world glimmers, fresh and bright,
As shadows fade to morning light.
Every blade of grass aglow,
In this magic, hearts will grow.

A canvas painted with delight,
Beneath a sky so pure and white.
Breath of wind, a tender touch,
The dawn's embrace, we love so much.

Watch as day begins to bloom,
In this bright and sacred room.
The crystal spectacle unfolds,
With secrets of the dawn retold.

## **The Hush of Morn's Kiss**

Silent whispers greet the day,
The night's shadows melt away.
Softly now, the world awakes,
In the calm, a breath it takes.

Colors blend in gentle light,
Painting scenes both sheer and bright.
In the stillness, dreams take flight,
Morning's kiss, pure and slight.

Crisp air dances around our skin,
As nature whispers, "Let's begin."
Every moment, fresh and new,
The beat of life, a quiet cue.

Clouds roll by, a fleeting sight,
As warmth spills down in golden light.
Hearts align with nature's song,
In this hush, we all belong.

Time surrenders to the morn,
In soft whispers, love is born.
The hush of dawn, a sacred space,
Where hope finds its timeless place.

## Frosted Petals of the New Day

Frosted petals greet the dawn,
Glistening jewels on the lawn.
Nature wears her crystal crown,
In the light, she won't back down.

Every leaf a sparkling gem,
Sunrise warms the fragile stem.
Beauty blooms in chilly air,
Whispers promise everywhere.

As the day begins to rise,
Mirrors of the morning skies.
Promises shine with every ray,
Frosted petals lead the way.

Birds awaken, take their flight,
Dancing in the morning light.
Gentle breezes start to play,
In laughter, we find our way.

Every moment brings a gift,
Nature's hand, a gentle lift.
Frosty charms of the new day,
In our hearts, they'll ever stay.

## **Luminous Icy Veils**

Icy veils like whispering dreams,
Cascade down in shimmering streams.
Nature's breath, a frozen sigh,
Underneath the glowing sky.

Crystals form on every space,
Glistening bright, a soft embrace.
In the stillness, secrets held,
Winter's magic, gently spelled.

Moonlit nights and frosty eves,
Wrap the earth in silver leaves.
Every corner, beauty found,
Guided by a soft, sweet sound.

Luminous glow lights the way,
All in peace, we wish to stay.
In this wonder, hearts ignite,
Through the veil, we find the light.

As dawn breaks, the ice will melt,
But each moment, deeply felt.
Luminous icy veils unfold,
Tales of winter softly told.

## Chilly Fingers of Daylight

The dawn creeps soft and slow,
With fingers cold and bright,
It brushes all below,
A canvas painted white.

Trees wear their crystal coats,
As shadows gently fade,
The world, in silence, floats,
In morning's tender shade.

A breath of icy air,
Wraps around the waking earth,
Each moment laid bare,
Whispers of a new birth.

The sky blushes in pink,
As sun's rays start to weave,
Through branches, we can think,
Of all the dreams we leave.

So let the daylight tease,
With chills that spark delight,
In early morning's freeze,
Chilly fingers hold us tight.

## Shivering Reflections in the Morning

In the stillness of dawn,
Mirrors of frost appear,
Glistening like a yawn,
Whispering winter near.

The pond wears a still guise,
Reflecting skies so clear,
As vapor starts to rise,
The day begins to cheer.

Leaves tremble in the breeze,
Shivering with delight,
Nature's quiet tease,
In the soft morning light.

Each ray a gentle brush,
On a canvas defined,
Creating such a hush,
In the landscape entwined.

We walk in wonder's grip,
With breaths that kiss the air,
Each moment we equip,
With joy beyond compare.

## The Magic Threads of Frost

A tapestry unfolds,
As winter weaves its thread,
With silver, blue, and gold,
On everything it's spread.

The grass, a jeweled field,
Each blade a work of art,
Nature's grace revealed,
As frost plays its sweet part.

Trees twinkling with delight,
Like crystals in the sun,
Boundless beauty in sight,
A magic dance begun.

Each branch, a woven lace,
Embraced by morning's chill,
Transforming every space,
With elegance and will.

As sun begins to rise,
Threads warm the frozen ground,
In the spin of skies,
Magic all around.

# Frost's Gentle Whisper to the Day

Frost speaks in hushed tones,
A serenade to the morn,
In glimmers and in stones,
A chill that feels reborn.

Whispers glide on the breeze,
Through the woodland so fair,
Every leaf has its tease,
In nature's frosty air.

The sunrise kisses cold,
With warmth that breaks the spell,
In colors bright and bold,
Where frosty secrets dwell.

Each moment slowly wakes,
From slumber's icy grasp,
With every breath we take,
In joy's gentle clasp.

Frost's touch is a message,
Of beauty's fleeting way,
In this soft passage,
It welcomes in the day.

## **Shards of Ice and Morning Glow**

Beneath the dawn, the ice does gleam,
Fragments sparkle, like a dream.
Each shard reflects the morning light,
A delicate dance, pure and bright.

Chill whispers call on frosty air,
Nature wakes with gentle care.
Time stands still in this embrace,
As shadows fade without a trace.

The world adorned in crystalline,
A fleeting beauty, so divine.
With each new ray, the warmth will rise,
Transforming shards to soft blue skies.

Echoes of winter softly sigh,
As daylight breathes, the chill will die.
In moments brief, we seize the glow,
Remembering shards of ice below.

## The Stillness Before Warmth

In silence deep, the world awaits,
The dawn approaches, opening gates.
A breath of frost hangs in the air,
Before the warmth, there's stillness rare.

The earth is cloaked in a silver sheet,
Nature holds its heartbeat sweet.
The upcoming sun, a promise, bold,
As secrets of the night unfold.

Each moment lingers, time stands still,
Anticipation, a quiet thrill.
Colder whispers brush the ground,
Where life and light will soon abound.

As shadows blend with morning's hue,
The stillness breaks, and life renews.
With gentle warmth, the day will start,
Awakening joy within each heart.

## Frostbitten Dreams Unraveled

In the tranquil hush of frosty night,
Dreams lie waiting, out of sight.
Beneath the ice, they softly glow,
Frostbitten whispers, lost in snow.

Each dream encased in crystal hold,
Stories of warmth yet to be told.
With every breath, they dance and sigh,
Tales of warmth beneath the sky.

As winter's grip begins to fade,
Hope unfurls, no longer stayed.
Unraveling threads of icy seams,
Awakening softly, like spring dreams.

From frozen silence, new hopes arise,
As light spills forth and cold defies.
Frostbitten dreams now set them free,
Embraced by warmth, a symphony.

## Morning's Icy Embrace

The morning breaks with icy hands,
Wrapping the world in frosted bands.
Each breath a vapor, crisp and clear,
In morning's grasp, the chill draws near.

A hushed serenade of sparkling light,
Glittering whispers, pure and bright.
Nature dons her icy attire,
A beauty born from winter's fire.

In every corner, silence reigns,
While sunlight kisses frozen chains.
Colors shift as warmth awakes,
In morning's hold, the stillness breaks.

Yet for a moment, we embrace
The lingering chill, this magic space.
For soon the thaw will bring release,
And morning's touch will bring us peace.

## Reflections of a Chilled Awakening

In the dawn's pale light,
Shadows dance on the ground,
Whispers of night take flight,
As warmth starts to abound.

Dewdrops cling to the grass,
Glistening like lost dreams,
Each moment seems to pass,
Softly in gentle streams.

Silent echoes around,
Nature's breath held so still,
A world yet to be found,
Awaits the morning's thrill.

The frost bites at my toes,
Yet I feel strangely free,
In this calm, still repose,
I find serenity.

A heartbeat starts to rise,
With the sun's golden gleam,
And as I open my eyes,
I kiss the quiet dream.

# Dreams Woven in Frost

In the quiet of night,
Dreams are spun with cold thread,
Stars twinkle with delight,
As whispers of frost are fed.

Silvery lace takes flight,
Over fields where shadows play,
Transforming the mundane sight,
Into a bright ballet.

Every flake is a wish,
Floating softly in the air,
Each breath turns to a mist,
In this moment, so rare.

Underneath the moon's gaze,
Secrets lie in the white,
Frostbite's soft embrace,
Holds magic in the night.

Awake in the stillness,
With a heart full of dreams,
Wrapped in nature's chillness,
Life's beauty brightly gleams.

## **Frostbitten Blossoms**

Amidst the winter's chill,
Blossoms brave the bitter frost,
With petals soft and still,
They flourish, never lost.

Snows blanket their grace,
While sunlight fights to break through,
Nature's warm embrace,
Nurtures life in shades of blue.

They bloom against the cold,
A testament to the will,
Every hue bright and bold,
Holds beauty time can't kill.

Though icy winds may blow,
Their colors fiercely glow,
In the heart of winter's show,
Hope's tender seeds they sow.

Frostbitten yet so strong,
Each flower tells a tale,
Of resilience lifelong,
In the face of every gale.

## **The Hush Before the Sun**

In the twilight's embrace,
A stillness fills the air,
Night drapes its silken lace,
Over dreams beyond compare.

Stars begin their slow fade,
As shadows merge with light,
A soft serenade,
Whispers secrets of the night.

The world holds its breath tight,
Waiting for warmth to creep,
Nature stirs in the slight,
Awakening from deep sleep.

The chilly breeze dances,
Caressing each tree's limb,
With each moment, time prances,
In a quiet, tender hymn.

Soon the sun will arise,
Chasing darkness away,
But in this hush, the skies,
Share a promise of the day.

## The Merge of Ice and Dawn

In the stillness of the night,
Where shadows softly creep,
Ice meets the first light's touch,
Awakening dreams from sleep.

Crystals shimmer on the ground,
Mirroring the sun's embrace,
Colors blend in gentle breaths,
Painting nature's hidden grace.

A fusion bright and bold,
Chasing away the dark,
Each drop of dew tells tales,
Of magic's gentle spark.

As dawn unfurls its wings,
The world begins to sing,
In harmony of warmth and chill,
Nature's joy in everything.

The ice gives way to golden hues,
A dance of light and shade,
In the melting hearts of morn,
New beginnings are made.

## **Whispers of Winter's Light**

A canvas white with icy breath,
In silence, winter speaks,
Each flake a gentle promise,
Carried on the wind's cheeks.

Beneath the silvered canopy,
Soft shadows start to play,
Whispers of the light above,
Guiding night to day.

Crystalline structures glisten bright,
Reflecting hopes anew,
In every glimmer and every spark,
Life bursts through with dew.

Echoes of the frosty breeze,
Dance among the trees,
A symphony of winter's grace,
Carries life with ease.

So in the chill, find warmth inside,
As magic weaves its art,
In whispers soft, winter reveals,
The beauty of the heart.

## **Crystal Veils of Morning**

Mornings draped in crystal veils,
Whispering tales of the night,
Breath of frost upon the ground,
In a dance of sheer delight.

The sun breaks through the icy mist,
Casting diamonds on the grass,
Every blade a work of art,
A moment meant to last.

Nature wakes with gentle grace,
Awash in soft embrace,
In the quiet, life unfolds,
A tender, timeless space.

Birds awaken with sweet songs,
Filling air with joyful sound,
Each note a kiss of warmth bestowed,
As the world spins round.

In crystal veils, the day takes flight,
Imbued with hope anew,
Morning's light, a faithful guide,
In every shade and hue.

## The Chill of Awakening

Awake to winter's gentle grip,
The chill wraps every soul,
As nature breathes its frosty breath,
In a moment, pure and whole.

Every sigh of morning air,
Carries whispers of the day,
The earth unveils its frosted heart,
In a soft, enchanting way.

Beneath the stars, a world reborn,
Where silence softly reigns,
Each breath a cloud of fleeting time,
Marking nature's endless chains.

With every rise of sunlit hue,
The chill begins to fade,
As warmth unfurls its tender wings,
Promising joys remade.

The chill of awakening sings,
Of life beneath the frost,
In every crystal's gleaming light,
All burdens become lost.

## A Beautiful Chill in the Air

A whisper flows through the trees,
Cool and gentle, a soft tease.
Leaves shiver, dances in flight,
Embracing the morning's light.

The world wears a frosty gown,
Nature's beauty, a jeweled crown.
Breath of winter, crisp and clear,
Inviting us to draw near.

Silence blankets the sleepy ground,
The only sound is joy unbound.
Children play, laughter does soar,
In the chill, spirits explore.

Twinkling stars fade with the dawn,
Each ray stretched, as night is drawn.
Embers of warmth blend with the cold,
Each moment again retold.

In this perfect season's grace,
We find our hearts find their place.
With every breath, we feel alive,
In the chill, our spirits thrive.

## **Ethereal Frost and Sunlight's Kiss**

Morning breaks, a sight so rare,
Frosty jewels in the air.
Sunlight's kiss warms the chill,
Filling hearts with gentle thrill.

Patterns dance on windowpanes,
Nature's art with no remains.
Each sparkle tells a story new,
Awakening the world in hue.

Footprints pressed on powdered white,
Marking journeys, pure delight.
With laughter shared and warmth in view,
Life unfolds in shades of blue.

Clouds drift softly, shadows play,
As the warm sun paves the way.
In every heartbeat, hope does rise,
Ethereal moments, painted skies.

In this cascade of light and shade,
Happiness in each upgrade.
A dance of seasons, bright and clear,
In the frost, we find our cheer.

## The Gentle Caress of Chilly Light

Winter's breath, so soft and sweet,
Gentle caress of seasonal greet.
The sky aglow in twilight's embrace,
Each moment crafted, a tender space.

Pine trees whisper to the breeze,
Nature rests, finds its ease.
The starkness of branches, a painter's brush,
In every corner, the world does hush.

Icicles hang with grace and pride,
Glistening cool, nature's wide glide.
Underneath the blanket of snow,
Lies a warmth, ready to grow.

Winds sing tales of days gone by,
As the sun begins to shy.
The twilight dances, shadows grow,
In the cold, hidden gems glow.

Hold tight to the magic it brings,
In this chill, our spirit sings.
Wrapped in light, we find our way,
A gentle caress, come what may.

## The Breathe of a Frozen Dawn

Awake anew, the dawn ignites,
Painting the sky with soft delights.
A frozen breath, crisp and pure,
Every moment feels mature.

Glistening fields, a blanket wide,
Softened earth with dreams inside.
The sun peeks through, a gentle sigh,
In its warmth, the shadows die.

Birds take flight, a graceful song,
Welcoming day that feels so strong.
With every flap, a promise bright,
Morning whispers, claiming light.

The frost retreats, with grace it leaves,
Every branch dressed, nature weaves.
In the tender glow of dawn's glare,
We find our spirits rise in air.

Hold tight to this path of gold,
In the frozen sun, stories told.
A breathe of day, fresh and bright,
In every heartbeat, pure delight.

## Awakening in a Winter Gaze

Morning whispers through the frost,
Trees stand still, their warmth now lost.
A blanket white, the world asleep,
In silence, winter's beauty we keep.

Crystalline jewels catch the light,
Each branch adorned, a wondrous sight.
The breath of nature, sharp and clear,
Awakening dreams, drawing near.

Footprints trace where shadows blend,
In this stillness, time can bend.
Whispers of the past remain,
In frozen moments, never vain.

Colors shimmer in the frost,
A vibrant canvas, never lost.
Life stirs beneath the icy veil,
In winter's grip, stories prevail.

Awakening the heart's delight,
In every breath, a spark ignites.
A journey through a stark embrace,
Winter's gaze, a sacred space.

## **Shimmering Hues of Dawn**

A canvas painted soft and bright,
Whispers of dawn take their flight.
Crimson blushes kiss the skies,
Dreams awaken, as daylight sighs.

Shimmering hues stretch far and wide,
Where secrets of the night abide.
Morning's glow on shadows creep,
A promise made, the world to keep.

Colors dance as daylight swells,
In harmony, nature tells.
With every hue, a story spun,
Life rekindles with the sun.

Birds take flight in joyous song,
As daybreak's light brings them along.
Awake, the flowers gently sway,
In shimmering hues, find your way.

As the sun climbs, shadows play,
Painting warmth in shades of gray.
In every moment, grace bestowed,
Shimmering hues, the heart's abode.

**Frozen Breath of Daybreak**

A chill in the air, the day begins,
Frosted whispers where silence spins.
Each breath visible, like dreams of night,
Frozen magic, capturing light.

Morning breaks with a crystal song,
As the world stretches, it won't be long.
The sun peeks through, a gentle tease,
Awakening warmth with a soft breeze.

Ice glistens on branches high,
A fleeting moment, a gentle sigh.
Nature's art, intricate and bold,
Stories of winter patiently told.

The horizon blushes, shadows lift,
In frozen breath, a precious gift.
Every moment, a chance to see,
The beauty wrapped in winter's spree.

As day unfolds, the stillness fades,
Life stirs beneath, where warmth cascades.
The frozen breath of daybreak speaks,
In every moment, the spirit seeks.

## **Echoes of a Cold Rising Sun**

In the distance, a brightening glow,
Echoes of warmth start to flow.
Through frosty air, the sun takes hold,
Shining down on landscapes bold.

Cold fingers of night slowly recede,
Awakening life, a gentle lead.
Each ray ignites a spark anew,
In echoes, the world begins to renew.

Silence breaks with the dawn's embrace,
Softly, shadows return to their place.
Nature listens, ready to rise,
As a cold sun paints brightening skies.

Winds whisper secrets to trees so tall,
In quiet beauty, we hear their call.
The echoes of light, a promise to keep,
With a breath of warmth, we gently leap.

As day stretches forth, we stand in awe,
Of the rising sun with a radiant draw.
Echoes linger, sweet melodies spun,
In the heart of the cold, we embrace the sun.

## The Silence of Frosted Hours

In the chill of morning light,
A blanket of silence laid soft,
Crystal whispers kiss the ground,
Where shadows of winter drift aloft.

Frosted dreams hold their breath,
Each moment a frozen sigh,
Stillness wraps the world around,
As time whispers a gentle goodbye.

Pale blue skies, a distant call,
As daylight begins to unfold,
A tapestry of sparkling white,
In stories waiting to be told.

Echoes of winter's embrace,
In the hush of dawn's soft glow,
Nature holds its secrets close,
As the frost begins to show.

The silence of these frosted hours,
Breathes a magic, rare and bright,
In every twinkle, every glance,
A moment wrapped in pure delight.

## **Delicate Frost on Awakening Blooms**

In gardens where dreams arise,
Delicate frost rests with care,
On petals ripe with morning dew,
Whispering secrets in the air.

Sunlight dances on cold blades,
As life starts to stretch and wake,
Each bloom adorned in crystalline,
A testament of the heart's ache.

Colors emerge in quiet grace,
Through foggy whispers they bloom,
A kaleidoscope of fresh hope,
As winter begins to resume.

Nature paints with gentle strokes,
Frost and warmth entwined in play,
Awaiting the kiss of sunlight,
To melt dreams of winter away.

Awakening blooms rise anew,
In the light of a thawing day,
Wrapped in the whispers of frost,
As the seasons dance and sway.

## **Chilled Light Breaking Through**

The dawn breaks with a gentle chill,
Light glimmers on the icy lake,
Soft shadows stretch to greet the sun,
As winter starts to slowly wake.

Whispers of frost cling to trees,
Boughs adorned in glittering lace,
The air, crisp with unspoken words,
Holds the beauty of this space.

Sunbeams pierce the heavy veil,
In a tango of warmth and cold,
Illuminating nature's art,
A canvas of stories untold.

The world is alight with promise,
As shadows begin to retreat,
Chilled light shimmering through branches,
A symphony, gentle and sweet.

In this fleeting, tender hour,
Hope rises with the morning dew,
Embracing each fragile moment,
As chilled light breaks brightly through.

## A Glisten in the Early Sky

A glisten hangs in the early sky,
As dawn unfolds its golden hue,
Stars bow out with blushing grace,
And night bids a soft adieu.

Clouds embrace the sun's warm rays,
In a dance of light and shadow,
A whisper of dreams caught in time,
Painting paths where hearts may flow.

Birds awaken with tranquil songs,
Filling the air with joyful flight,
As the world stirs from its slumber,
In the sweetness of morning light.

Moments linger in the stillness,
Where thoughts of yesterday stray,
A glisten in the early sky,
Brings promise of a new day.

With each breath of this brand new morn,
Hope rises upon soft wings,
In the glisten of the early sky,
The heart sings what the spirit brings.

## A Quiet Rebirth of Light

In dawn's embrace, shadows flee,
New warmth whispers softly, free.
The world awakens, breath anew,
In gentle hues, the colors grew.

Birds sing sweetly, tunes that tease,
Nature dances in the breeze.
Morning's blush upon the hill,
A quiet joy, the heart to fill.

Raindrops glisten, diamonds bright,
Reflecting hope, a pure delight.
Each petal blooms, the earth does sigh,
Underneath this endless sky.

Laughter echoes, bright and clear,
The day begins, the path draws near.
In harmony, the spirit lifts,
A masterpiece, creation gifts.

With every glow, the night lets go,
A tender moment, soft and slow.
In tranquil peace, we find our part,
A rebirth felt within the heart.

## **Delicate Patterns in Stillness**

Amidst the hush, a pattern sways,
In quiet realms, the heart obeys.
Whispers weave through tranquil air,
A dance of dreams, both light and rare.

The silver moon adorns the night,
Casting shadows, soft and bright.
Each star twinkles, stories told,
In delicate grace, the night unfolds.

Gentle ripples on water's face,
Reflecting time, a fleeting grace.
Nature's brush stroke, fine and thin,
In stillness, life begins within.

Petals fall like whispered words,
Silent songs of unseen birds.
Threads of fate, they intertwine,
Creating beauty, yours and mine.

As dawn unveils its golden thread,
With vibrant hues, the silence fled.
In every moment, patterns gleam,
A tapestry, a waking dream.

## **Shimmering Skies of Early Light**

The morning breaks, a canvas wide,
With colors washed, the stars collide.
Golden rays spill from the sun,
Painting dreams where shadows run.

Clouds drift softly in pastel hues,
Whispering secrets to the dews.
A symphony of light and air,
In harmony, the day lays bare.

Each breeze carries scents so sweet,
As nature wakes beneath our feet.
The world, aglow with hopes of gold,
As tales of life begin to unfold.

Sparkling twilight, dusk arrives,
Where every heartbeat gently strives.
In shimmering skies, the dreams take flight,
Guided by the soft moonlight.

With every glow, the heart ignites,
In tranquil whispers, endless sights.
Embrace the dawn, let spirits rise,
In shimmering hues, we find our ties.

## The Frost's Gentle Caress

A quiet morn, the world is still,
With icy breath, the air does chill.
Shimmering crystals, nature's lace,
Each branch adorned, a frosty grace.

Footsteps crunch on the frozen ground,
In this stillness, beauty's found.
Whispers of winter paint the scene,
In silent white, the world serene.

Soft sunlight filters, warm and bright,
Turning frost into diamonds light.
Nature's canvas, crisp and clear,
With every sparkle, warmth draws near.

Breathe in deep, the frosty air,
A moment's peace beyond compare.
In gentle caress, the cold bestows,
A quiet touch as winter glows.

Embrace the chill, let silence reign,
In winter's arms, we feel no pain.
For even in the coldest day,
The heart can find its bright display.

## Morning's Chilling Embrace

Whispers of dawn greet the day,
Breath of winter in the air.
Shadows dance in muted gray,
While dreams linger everywhere.

Silence holds the world so tight,
As frost paints the ground with care.
Each blade sparkles, pure and bright,
A crystal maze with chill to share.

Birds begin their softest song,
A tune to wake the sleepy earth.
In the hush, we all belong,
Finding comfort in rebirth.

Golden rays will soon appear,
Chasing frost from every lane.
Yet in this moment clear,
We embrace the cold's sweet reign.

## The Frosty Embrace of First Light

Morning breaks with chilling breath,
A quiet hush upon the land.
Frosty whispers hint at death,
Yet life stirs with gentle hand.

Each branch wears a gleaming coat,
Nature's artistry on show.
Time drifts by, a drifting boat,
In the soft and silent glow.

Colors bloom in muted tones,
As daylight starts to softly creep.
In this realm where magic hones,
The world awakens from its sleep.

Breathe in deep this tranquil scene,
The cold, a friend as day is born.
In the chill, beauty's sheen,
Casts a spell, a fragile morn.

## **Glistening Tranquility Awaits**

The stillness holds the bitter cold,
A canvas fresh with nature's art.
Each sparkle tells a tale retold,
Of peacefulness that fills the heart.

Softly, light begins to dance,
A ballet of the dawn's embrace.
In that moment, we find chance,
To savor stillness, find our place.

Glistening dreams upon the grass,
Each droplet holds a world inside.
In these moments, fears can pass,
As beauty flows like a gentle tide.

This tranquil morn, a sacred space,
Awaits all souls that seek to breathe.
In shadows' grace, we find our pace,
And weave our dreams, our hearts to wreathe.

## Lacy Intricacies of Dawn

Awake to threads of silver lace,
Embroidered on the waking earth.
Nature crafts a soft embrace,
In the silence, we find worth.

Each frost-kissed leaf, a work of art,
Delicate in morning's glow.
Whispers rise from nature's heart,
Cradling dreams that slowly grow.

As the sun peeks, shy yet bold,
The lace begins to melt away.
In its warmth, new tales unfold,
Crafted in the light of day.

Celebrate the gentle show,
Of dawn's dance, a perfect start.
In the threads of light we know,
Lies the beauty, love, and art.

## **A Gilded Touch of Cold**

The whispering chill, a soft embrace,
Crystals glisten on nature's face.
Golden rays in frosty air,
Winter's breath, beyond compare.

A silver sheen on branches bare,
Dancing jewels, a dreamlike flare.
Each moment caught in glint and glow,
A gilded touch as breezes blow.

Footsteps crunch on icy ground,
Echoes of a season found.
In this temple of crisp delight,
Cold wraps softly, sheer and light.

Bitter sweetness fills the sky,
Nature whispers a soft sigh.
Wrapped in layers, warmth bestows,
A gilded world where wonder grows.

As daylight fades, the shadows creep,
In frozen art, the silence deep.
A gilded touch embraces night,
Cold and soft, a heart's delight.

## **Specters of a Silver Morning**

In dawn's embrace, the silver light,
Whispers weave through the quiet night.
Shadows dance 'neath the misty glow,
Specters rise, a ghostly show.

Frosted breath on window pane,
Echoes of dreams, joy and pain.
Gentle hues of gray and white,
Morning shrouded in soft twilight.

The world emerges, fresh and bright,
Nature's canvas, pure delight.
Birds take wing in swirling air,
Feel the magic everywhere.

Every step, the earth does sing,
Nature's heart, a fragile thing.
Silver morning, softly bold,
Stories whispered, tales untold.

In this realm where spirits play,
Time stands still, then fades away.
Specters linger to greet the day,
In silken light, we find our way.

## **When Silence Wears White**

When silence wears a cloak of white,
Worlds transform in soft twilight.
Snowflakes drift, a gentle treat,
Whispers hush as soft winds meet.

Branches bow in reverent grace,
Nature pauses in this space.
Each flake tells of peace and calm,
Echoing a winter's balm.

Footprints mar the pristine sheet,
Moments frozen, bittersweet.
As time flows like a river still,
Silent dreams on a distant hill.

In this hush, the heart can hear,
Echoes soft as stars draw near.
When silence wears white, we find,
A tranquil space for heart and mind.

As twilight dims, the shadows creep,
In snowy white, our secrets keep.
When silence wears its blanket deep,
In the cold, our souls take leap.

## **Luminous Frost Unfolding**

In the dawn, a shimmer gleams,
Luminous frost, life's gentle dreams.
Each crystal bright in morning's glow,
Nature's art begins to show.

Grass adorned in icy lace,
Whispers secrets that time won't trace.
The world awakes with tender sighs,
As frosty breath paints winter skies.

Every leaf a glinting star,
Beauty found, both near and far.
The sun breaks through, a golden hue,
Revealing wonders, fresh and new.

In this realm of sparkling white,
Frost unfolds with pure delight.
Softly gliding, moments pass,
Time encased in icy glass.

When evening falls, the light retreats,
Stars emerge, the pulse repeats.
Luminous frost, a fleeting show,
In tranquil night, the magic flows.

## **Gleaming Frost Beneath the Sky**

Glistening crystals on the ground,
Whispers of winter all around.
Moonlight dances on icy streams,
A world wrapped up in frosty dreams.

Trees adorned in silver lace,
Silent beauty finds its place.
Each step crunches underfoot,
Nature's quiet, soft and mute.

Stars twinkle in the frosty night,
Guiding wanderers with their light.
A chill upon the evening air,
Magic floats, both rich and rare.

In the morning, sun will rise,
Painting warmth across the skies.
Yet for now, the stillness reigns,
Frosty jewel that nature gains.

The world pauses, breath held tight,
In the glow of pale moonlight.
Frozen wonders, softly gleam,
In this winter's perfect dream.

## **Traces of Winter's Breath**

Breezes soft with icy bite,
Whispers carried in the night.
Footprints left on frosty trails,
Marking moments, silent tales.

Snowflakes drift like whispered sighs,
Filling spaces 'neath grey skies.
Each flake dances, wild and free,
A tapestry of memory.

Branches bow with crystal weight,
Nature's art that holds our fate.
In the hush, a secret speaks,
Winter's breath, so cold, it seeks.

The world transforms, a pure white sheet,
Heartbeats quicken with the beat.
In the dawn, a promise glows,
A warmth beneath the frost that shows.

Once more will spring return to play,
But for now, in stillness stay.
Traces linger, soft and slow,
Memories of the winter's glow.

## **Ethereal Hues of Dawn**

Colors burst, a vivid spread,
Gold and pink where dreams are fed.
Light creeps in, dispelling night,
Awakening the world to light.

Birds begin their morning song,
Nature hums, the day feels strong.
Rays of sun touch every leaf,
In this canvas, joy is brief.

Dewdrops cling to blades of grass,
Sparkling gems, they come to pass.
Each moment filled with gentle grace,
Ethereal hues that time can trace.

Clouds of lavender drift and play,
Chasing shadows far away.
Dawn's embrace, a tender kiss,
Filling hearts with purest bliss.

Wonders wait beneath the sky,
In the stillness, dreams can fly.
Eternal whispers softly drawn,
In the hues of sweetened dawn.

## Glistening Silence Breaks

The hush of night begins to fade,
Morning's promise, softly made.
Awakening the sleeping earth,
Whispers of the day's rebirth.

Light cascades through window panes,
Chasing shadows, breaking chains.
Stillness breaks with laughter's sound,
In the glow, new joys are found.

Glistening dew on petals lie,
Kissed by dawn's embrace on high.
Nature stretches, yawns awake,
Every moment, pure joy makes.

Branches sway in gentle breeze,
Rustling songs through morning trees.
Warmth ignites the world anew,
Painting skies in vibrant hue.

In the meadow, colors burst,
Life awakens, quenched our thirst.
Glistening silence fades away,
In the light of a brand new day.

## Morning Frost's Soft Serenade

Morning light shimmers bright,
A frosty veil, pure and white.
Whispers dance on gentle air,
Nature's song, beyond compare.

Each blade glistens with despair,
Sunrise kisses everywhere.
Each breath puffs a cloud of fog,
Serenity, like a warm hug.

Footsteps crunch on chilly grass,
Through the woods, the moments pass.
Birds awaken, crisp and clear,
Softly singing, drawing near.

Winds caress the frozen ground,
In stillness, magic's found.
Every shadow, a work of art,
Morning frost, a brand new start.

As the day begins to rise,
Hope awakens in the skies.
Warmth will melt this icy glow,
But for now, let the beauty flow.

## Awash in Chilling Luminance

Glare of light on frosted trees,
Winter's breath in gentle breeze.
Silence wrapped in shimmering white,
Awash in chilling brilliance, bright.

Colors fade, yet shine so bold,
Stories captured, yet untold.
Clouds drift slowly, laced with grace,
In this chill, a warm embrace.

Steps leave patterns on the ground,
Echoes of a silent sound.
Nature's jewels adorn the earth,
In this moment, find rebirth.

Time stands still in morning's glow,
Underneath the silver show.
Every nook, a peaceful sight,
Awash in pure, enchanting light.

But as noon begins to creep,
Warmth will flow, and shadows sleep.
Cherish now this quiet stay,
Let this chilling magic play.

## The Elegance of Frosted Mornings

Veils of frost on window panes,
Whisper softly, nature's refrains.
Crystals twinkle, shining bright,
In the hush of early light.

Every breath a misty dream,
Nature's beauty in the gleam.
Glistening patterns, nature's hand,
In this calm, we understand.

Sunrise paints with golden hues,
An artist's palette, bright and true.
Winter's grasp, a gentle hold,
In the cold, warm stories unfold.

With each step, the world awakes,
A symphony of tiny flakes.
Grace and peace in every scene,
In this frosted world, serene.

As the day moves on its way,
Embracing warmth, the frost will sway.
But in memory, it will stay,
Elegance of a frozen day.

## Whispered Secrets of the Glacial Rise

Mountains crowned with icy grace,
Whispers speak in silent space.
Glacial tongues of azure flow,
Hidden wonders, deep below.

Rivers freeze but hearts ignite,
In the glow of winter's light.
Secrets buried under snow,
Only nature's whispers know.

Each flake falls, a story spun,
In the twilight, day is done.
Frosted dreams on frosty nights,
Magic gleams in silver lights.

Hope is found in frozen streams,
In this glacial realm of dreams.
Tender moments, soft and sweet,
Whispered secrets, hearts will meet.

As dawn breaks, the chill shall fade,
But the memories won't evade.
In every frost, a tale resides,
Whispered secrets, winter's tides.

## **Glimmering Secrets of Daybreak**

Whispers of dawn kiss the sky,
Stars fade as dreams slowly die.
Golden rays pierce the night,
Revealing the world in soft light.

Birds awaken with gentle calls,
Nature celebrates, life enthralls.
Shadows retreat, horizons glow,
Unraveling secrets the night won't show.

A canvas painted, fresh and new,
Each moment holds a vibrant hue.
With every heartbeat, colors bloom,
Embracing the warmth, dispelling gloom.

Silent echoes of yesterday's dreams,
Merge with the dawn in radiant beams.
Hope rises, clad in bright array,
Cradled gently in the arms of day.

Glimmers of life springing awake,
In the embrace of daylight's break.
Each heartbeat a promise, softly spoken,
A tapestry of dawn, unbroken.

## **A Frozen Symphony of Dawn**

Frosted whispers touch the ground,
In silence, beauty spins around.
Each crystal glimmers, pure and bright,
A frozen symphony greets the light.

Nature wraps herself in white,
Quietly celebrating the night.
With each breath, the world exhales,
As sunlight weaves through icy trails.

Melodies drift on the chilly air,
Awakening dreams that linger there.
Harmony spreads, frost in a dance,
Inviting twirls, a fleeting chance.

The sun begins its warm ascent,
Melted patterns, a life well-spent.
Icy shards reflect its glow,
In this moment, magic flows.

With every note, the dawn professes,
Nature's art, in pure caresses.
A frozen symphony fades away,
As colorful hues welcome the day.

## Morning's Chilled Artwork

Canvas of dawn, brushed in frost,
Colors whisper where all is lost.
Gentle strokes of pastel's embrace,
Each breath revealing a sacred space.

Chilled air dances with quiet glee,
Capturing moments, wild and free.
The sun peeks over the hill's crest,
Crafting a masterpiece from the rest.

Dewdrops shimmer on blades of grass,
Reflecting light as moments pass.
Nature's palette, vividly spun,
In harmony with the rising sun.

Birdsong mingles with morning's glow,
Awakening dreams, soft and slow.
The world exhales, a new day drawn,
A chilled artwork of the dawn.

Wonders unfold with each new ray,
Life reborn in vibrant display.
Morning's chill wraps around our hearts,
As tomorrow beckons, a fresh start.

## **Shivering Skies of Early Light**

Skies awaken, shivering blue,
Sunlight peeks, a bright debut.
Hues of gold and silver blend,
As night's curtain begins to bend.

Chilled breezes carry whispers near,
Of morning's promise, crystal clear.
Each star trembles, bidding adieu,
To the day that begins anew.

Clouds dance lightly in vibrant hue,
Painting stories the morning drew.
A symphony played on nature's stage,
As daylight turns the turning page.

The horizon shimmers, softly shy,
As warmth kisses the lingering sky.
Colors ripple, a joyful sight,
In the embrace of early light.

With every pulse, the world awakes,
In shimmering hues, destiny shakes.
Life unfolds in the blush of dawn,
As shadows fade and hope grows strong.

## Shattered Dreams of a Chilly Day

Whispers of hope in the frozen air,
Fleeting visions drift in despair.
Promises made, now scattered and gray,
Lost in the echo of a chilling day.

Hollow laughter fades into the night,
Memories shiver, dimming the light.
What once was vibrant, now feels so far,
A dream that faded, a forgotten star.

Frostbitten wishes hang low like dew,
Winds of regret whisper tales so blue.
In the silence, a heartbeat remains,
Carrying shadows of long-lost gains.

Yet in the frost, a glimmer appears,
A reminder of joys, a mosaic of tears.
Though dreams are shattered, they still can gleam,
In the cold embrace of a warming dream.

So let the chill wrap me in its fold,
For within the ice, lies a story untold.
Each fragment of dream, a part of the play,
Shattered, yet beautiful, on a chilly day.

## **Lingering Shades of Icy Dawn**

The world awakens in hues of gray,
Morning whispers, the night pulls away.
Silhouettes shiver, cast from the moon,
Lingering shadows dance to a tune.

Every breath taken, a visible sigh,
Nature's palette, where shadows lie.
Chilled breaths mingle in frosty delight,
As dawn brushes softly, painting with light.

A canvas of frost on the empty ground,
Echoes of darkness, now softly unbound.
Each step leaves an imprint, delicate, faint,
Marking the earth where silence can paint.

Colors emerge as the sun finds its place,
In icy whispers, the light starts to trace.
Each moment lingers, gently unfolds,
As warmth kisses chill with stories untold.

So let this dawn hold the wisps of the night,
In shades that linger, both somber and bright.
For in icy embrace, new life begins,
As the dawn awakens and hope always wins.

## Sunlight's Dance on Frosty Pines

Sunlight kisses the tips of the trees,
Where frost clings tightly, caressed by the breeze.
Pines sway gently, adorned in white,
In a delicate dance, catching the light.

Each needle sparkles like diamonds in air,
The world transformed, a beauty rare.
Warmth weaves through the chill like a thread,
Stitching together the night and the bed.

Birds greet the morn with songs soft and sweet,
As sunlight bathes all where shadows once meet.
Frosty enchantments, a fragile display,
In the heart of winter, come out to play.

The ground glistens as if kissed by the stars,
Each step that we take feels closer to Mars.
Nature's ballet, a wondrous sight,
Crafted in silence, a moment of flight.

So let us rejoice in this magical show,
As sunlight dances and warm breezes blow.
For within the chill, there's a vibrant life,
A fleeting beauty, amidst daily strife.

## Crystalline Glow of the New Day

Morning unfolds with a crystalline glow,
Nature awakens, ready to show.
The world is wrapped in a shimmering veil,
As sunlight spills softly, a delicate trail.

Glistening branches, a spectacle bright,
Reflecting the promise of warmth and light.
This new day beckons, inviting us near,
In whispers of joy, banishing fear.

Each ray dances gently on frost-kissed ground,
In the quiet beauty, magic is found.
Droplets of sunshine, a golden embrace,
Transforming the world with a radiant grace.

So here we stand, in wonder anew,
As the crystalline glow paints all that we view.
With each breath taken, we feel the ascent,
Of hope and of love, ever-present, immense.

And as the day brightens, shadows will flee,
In the crystalline warmth, we feel truly free.
With open hearts, let the moments replay,
In the beautiful light of the new day.

## Subtle Radiance in Frost

Whispers of dawn on icy ground,
Frosted jewels in silence found.
Soft light dances through the trees,
A gentle touch that brings us ease.

Every crystal holds a spark,
In the stillness, there's a mark.
Nature's breath, a cool embrace,
In the quiet, we find grace.

Shadows mingle with soft light,
Transforming day into the night.
Colorless beauty, pure and bright,
A fleeting glimpse of nature's might.

Moments freeze, and time stands still,
Carried on the winter's chill.
In this serenity, we stand,
Feeling the warmth of soft, cool hands.

Glimmers fade as day will wane,
Yet beauty lingers like a refrain.
In the heart of frost, we find,
A gentle glow that soothes the mind.

## **Glimmers on a Silver Horizon**

On the edge where day collides,
Silver whispers, evening glides.
Threads of light in twilight sew,
Dreams unfurl in the afterglow.

Mountains wear a crown of stars,
Holding secrets from afar.
Each glimmer shares a silent tale,
Of distant lands and winds that sail.

Softly wrapped in night's embrace,
Gentle shadows start to trace.
Moonlit pathways call and weave,
Inviting wanderers to believe.

Colors fade but spirits rise,
Dancing 'neath the velvet skies.
In the hush, we hear a song,
That beckons us to wander long.

A promise waits in dusk's sweet breath,
Life awakens anew from death.
Every glimmer, pure delight,
Guiding souls through endless night.

## **Ice-Kissed Serenity**

In the stillness of a dream,
Frosted branches softly gleam.
Gentle breath of winter's kiss,
Wraps the world in quiet bliss.

A blanket white on slumbered ground,
Where echoes of the past are found.
Soft as whispers, the world around,
In this peace, our hearts unbound.

Every flake a story spun,
Underneath the pale, cold sun.
Nature's art, a silent grace,
Reflecting time's most tender face.

Stillness reigns, the heart takes flight,
Through the shadows, into the light.
In frozen ponds, reflections lure,
A tranquil spirit, serene and pure.

As twilight dips, the stars ignite,
In ice-kissed scenes, we find our light.
Wrapped in warmth of frozen night,
Together, we embrace the sight.

# Morning's Lament in White

Softly rising, dawn appears,
In the hush, it calms our fears.
Fields adorned in gentle light,
Morning's lament, pure and bright.

Snowflakes drift on zephyr's breath,
Whispering tales of quiet death.
A silent world, a canvas wide,
Painting grief where dreams reside.

Each breath a cloud in chilled air,
Echoes linger, silence shared.
Footsteps crunching on the ground,
In this stillness, peace is found.

Branches bow beneath the weight,
Nature's sorrow, calm our fate.
Threads of white that softly weave,
A tapestry of hope to grieve.

Yet in the chill, warmth can start,
Life's resilience, a healing art.
Morning's lament, a promise shines,
In every heart, a love defines.

# The First Breath of Winter's Day

Snowflakes gently fall, soft and white,
Blanketing the earth, a hush of night.
Trees stand still, dressed in quiet grace,
Winter's breath whispers, a cold embrace.

Morning light breaks, golden and clear,
Chasing shadows, drawing near.
Every breath visible, a foggy sigh,
Hope in the chill, as time passes by.

Carols of silence fill the air,
Nature's stillness, a sacred prayer.
Birds shyly awaken, a timid call,
A winter symphony, enchanting all.

Footsteps crunch on the frosty ground,
Each step a promise, a joy profound.
The world anew in icy delight,
Wrapped in warmth, a serene sight.

As twilight descends, the stars appear,
Winter's cloak brings the night near.
A world transformed in shadows and glow,
In winter's grip, we find hope to grow.

## Shivering Hues at Dawn

Dawn breaks softly, hues of blue,
Nature awakening, fresh and new.
Frost-kissed petals shimmer in light,
A canvas painted, pure and bright.

Whispers of color dance on the breeze,
Nudging the world from winter's freeze.
Birds take flight, tracing the sky,
As sunlight drips from heaven's eye.

Trees stretch tall, their limbs adorned,
With secrets of night, the day has sworn.
Each shadow lengthens, a fleeting time,
In winter's breath, a subtle rhyme.

Unfurling leaves, a promise made,
Against the chill, bright hopes cascade.
A symphony of warmth, soft and sweet,
Life's awakening, a rhythm complete.

Moments linger, as the sun climbs high,
Painting the earth, the sprawling sky.
In shivering hues, the dawn doth play,
Bringing whispers of a brand new day.

## A Tapestry of Frost and Light

Frost weaves patterns on windowpanes,
A delicate art where beauty reigns.
Glistening threads of silver and white,
Nature's canvas, a wondrous sight.

Sunrise spills over the glistening ground,
Weaving warmth where chill was found.
Each ray a brushstroke, bold and bright,
In a tapestry spun of frost and light.

Icicles shimmer, like crystal daggers,
Hanging in silence, the cold still staggers.
A breath held tight, in winter's embrace,
Time stands still in this sacred space.

The world transforms, soft sighs of grace,
As shadows dance in a gentle pace.
Each moment captured in icy delight,
This tapestry glows in the morning light.

Echoes of winter weave through the air,
Stitching together the land with care.
A quilt of color, both bold and slight,
In a world where frost meets the light.

## Glacial Whispers at Sunrise

Glacial whispers kiss the morning dew,
As dawn unfolds in shades anew.
Mountains stand guard, carved by time,
Their majesty wrapped in silence sublime.

The sun ascends, a golden crown,
Warming the chill that's settled down.
Each beam a promise, crystalline bright,
Turning the frost to jewels of light.

Nature listens, the world holds its breath,
In the stillness, life conquers death.
The whispers echo with tales untold,
Of glaciers past, and futures bold.

Trees shimmer softly, their branches dance,
In the glow of morning, a wondrous trance.
The landscape awakens, the night retreats,
Music of nature, a song that repeats.

As the sun rises high, shadows recede,
Embracing the warmth of winter's need.
Glacial whispers fade into day,
Leaving behind a world at play.

Milton Keynes UK
Ingram Content Group UK Ltd.
UKHW010228111224
452348UK00011B/575